Edinburgh
Reading Test 4

MANUAL
THIRD EDITION

Educational Assessment Unit,
University of Edinburgh

HODDER
EDUCATION
AN HACHETTE UK COMPANY

Orders: please contact Bookpoint Ltd, 130 Milton Park, Abingdon, Oxon OX14 4SB.
Telephone: (44) 01235 827720, Fax: (44) 01235 400454. Lines are open from 9.00 to 5.00,
Monday to Saturday, with a 24-hour message answering service.
You can also order through our website at www.hoddereducation.co.uk

British Library Cataloguing in Publication Data
A catalogue record for this title is available from the British Library

Second edition 2000
Third edition 2002

ISBN-13: 978 0 340 84674 2

Impression number   11
Year   2008

Typeset by Fakenham Photosetting Ltd, Fakenham, Norfolk.
Printed in Great Britain for Hodder Education, an Hachette UK Company,
338 Euston Road, London NW1 3BH, by Hobbs the Printers Ltd, Totton, Hampshire.

Contents

The Edinburgh Reading Tests

The **Edinburgh Reading Tests** form a series of standardised, semi-diagnostic tests for all school ages from 7:0 to 16:6. They are primarily designed for administration to groups, although they can also be used with individuals.

There are four tests in the series: **ERT1** for ages 7:0 to 9:0, **ERT2** for ages 8:6 to 10:6, **ERT3** for ages 10:0 to 12:6, and **ERT4** for ages 12:0 to 16:6. Each test is divided into four or more subtests, each designed to assess a different area of reading competence, and is intended to be administered in two sessions of 25–50 minutes, including practice questions. For each pupil, the test yields an individual profile of strengths and weaknesses in reading, as well as a standardised score and Reading Age.

All four **Edinburgh Reading Tests** have been revised and updated in the years since their first publication, and have come to be regarded as synonymous with thoroughness and quality in school-based reading assessment. The most recent (2001/2) revision programme has enabled full updating, redesign and reorigination of the test booklets, shortening **ERT2** and **ERT3**, and complete restandardisation of **ERT1–3**: most of the participating schools contributed data for **ERT 1**, **2** and **3**, giving broad continuity throughout the primary phase. For **ERT4**, the age range of the test has been extended to 16:6.

THE PURPOSE OF THE TESTS

The construction of these tests was undertaken in the belief that instruments of this kind, designed for use by teachers and requiring no special psychometric expertise in administration or in interpretation of results, can assist in the teaching of reading. Such tests can provide information that will help the teacher, whether organising group activities or attending to the special needs of an individual pupil. In the light of the test results she[1] can adapt teaching methods and choose teaching materials to remedy a weakness or build on a strength.

These tests are straightforward to administer and simple to mark, and will help the teacher to appreciate more clearly both the general attainment and the particular strengths and weaknesses of each pupil. They will also help the teacher to evaluate the success of her own teaching methods with respect to the whole or to special areas of reading.

It must be emphasised that the tests, while containing a wide variety of types of material, are *tests*, and should always be treated as such. They do not necessarily represent good *teaching* practice, and are not intended to be used as teaching material. In practice, teaching for the test is unlikely to be successful as no substantial difficulty is involved in coping with the item types. If it is successful, then it serves only to reduce the validity of the results. The tests should be used only as part of a carefully planned system of assessment, diagnosis and appropriate follow-up.

For every pupil, the teacher can obtain an overall score for the whole test, and a separate score for each subtest. The **overall score** gives a valid and reliable estimate of a pupil's reading behaviour sampled in the test. This score can be converted into a quotient relating the pupil's performance to that of the population to which he belongs. For **ERT4**, these tables are based on a representative sample of state schools in England and a group of schools in one area of Scotland. These same samples provided scales of reading ages for a limited range of scores.

Within each test, the **subtests** are aimed at measuring different aspects of reading competence relevant to the age range being tested. As a result, the subtests tend to be most relevant to pupils within the designated age range. For example, a pupil aged 14 who has a nominal reading age of, say, 11, may well not encounter the same difficulties found by an average-ability eleven-year-old taking the same test.

Since they consist of fewer items, the subtests do not give as reliable results as the whole test, but they do give a useful diagnostic pointer to an individual pupil's areas of relative strength and weakness in reading.

---

[1] For convenience and clarity, the teacher is referred to as 'she' and the pupil as 'he' throughout this manual.

The Edinburgh Reading Tests and the National Curriculum Attainment Target for Reading

The National Curriculum Attainment Target for Reading is organised in levels, at each of which the expected attainment of pupils is described by a *Level Description*. Each of these Level Descriptions takes the form of a performance criterion defining an area of knowledge, skill and/or understanding.

For the most part, these criteria are broadly defined, and the Attainment Target as a whole takes a wide view of development in reading. It encompasses not only the ability to read increasingly complex texts accurately and with understanding, but also, for instance, information retrieval strategies, awareness of the author's use of words, and the ability to respond to and talk about what has been read, expressing and justifying opinions and preferences.

Assessment of pupils' achievement in relation to these broad and varied criteria is necessarily different in many respects from that of the **Edinburgh Reading Tests** and other standardised tests of reading. As group tests designed for relatively quick administration and scoring, the **Edinburgh Reading Tests** are necessarily based on relatively brief and isolated activities and texts to which pupils respond in writing; National Curriculum assessments involve a wide range of whole texts to which pupils respond in a variety of different ways. The outcomes of the two are also different. National Curriculum assessment provides descriptive information about what children can and cannot do; the **Edinburgh Reading Tests** provide numerical scores which enable a pupil's achievement to be compared with a national average and with that of other pupils.

Despite these differences, there are ways in which the complementary assessment procedures can usefully be related. This is particularly the case at the level of the individual subtest scores provided by the **Edinburgh Reading Tests**.

The skills covered by these subtests represent aspects of development in reading which are not only significant in their own right, but which can also be seen as underpinning and contributing to the more broadly defined areas in the Attainment Target for reading. Such parallels mean that the pattern of strengths and weaknesses revealed by the **Edinburgh Reading Tests** subtests can throw light on a pupil's progression through National Curriculum levels of attainment. In particular, the more sharply focused **Edinburgh Reading Tests** provide information about some of the basic skills, without which the broader, more inclusive competencies described in the Attainment Target for reading cannot be achieved.

The Edinburgh Reading Tests and the 5–14 Curriculum Guidelines in Scotland

The Scottish National Guidelines for English Language identify four broad areas of the language curriculum – Listening, Talking, Reading and Writing – termed *attainment outcomes*. Within each outcome there are described a number of *strands* or aspects of learning (e.g. listening in groups, talking about experiences, reading for information, personal writing). Most strands have attached to them statements of minimum competency or *attainment targets* at six broad levels of development covering primary and early secondary education from age 5 to age 14 years.

Six strands, or aspects of learning, are defined for Reading:

- Reading for information
- Reading for enjoyment
- Reading to reflect on the writer's ideas and craft
- Awareness of genre (type of text)
- Reading aloud
- Knowledge about language

While there is no direct link between the **Edinburgh Reading Tests** subtests and the reading strands and attainment targets set out in the 5–14 programme, the skills and competences covered by the tests represent important aspects of pupils' overall linguistic development. For example, the ability to find, select and use information from a variety of sources partly depends on retention of significant details and comprehension of essential ideas. Similarly, a pupil cannot be expected to read regularly for enjoyment without the ability to read at a reasonable rate, to understand essential ideas, to use context as a guide to understanding and without having a suitable range of vocabulary.

Thus, while the 5–14 English Language Guidelines describe what a pupil at different stages can be expected to do in terms of the Reading outcome, the **Edinburgh Reading Tests** assess some of the basic skills without which the desired outcome could not be achieved.

Edinburgh Reading Test 4

Edinburgh Reading Test 4 comprises 94 questions, which are divided into five subtests. Note that these subtests are *not* separately timed. The test is designed to be completed in a single session of 45 minutes, with reminders at 15, 30 and 40 minutes. The questions are all in multiple-choice formats, of different types, which allows for rapid marking which is completely objective.

The five subtests consist of:

A – **Skimming:** 16 items designed to test ability to extract required information without reading the passage closely.

B – **Vocabulary:** 24 items designed to test understanding of the meanings of words.

C – **Reading for Facts:** 20 items designed to test ability to decide what a passage says, or doesn't say.

D – **Points of View:** 17 items designed to test ability to perceive the consistency of various points of view.

E – **Comprehension:** 17 items designed to test ability to draw conclusions of an inferential nature about various passages.

Administering the test

Each pupil requires a **test booklet**, a **pencil** and a **rubber**. Pupils write their answers on the question booklet. Please check in good time that you have sufficient numbers of booklets, pencils and rubbers for each class or group you will be testing. You will also require these instructions and a watch.

Distribute the test booklets, face up. The pupils should not open the booklets at this stage. When ready, ask the pupils to write in the details asked for on the front cover.

There is then a short practice section which contains three questions exemplifying some of the item formats which the pupils will meet in the test itself. The main purpose, however, is simply to show pupils how to record, and if necessary change, their answers in the question booklet. Say:

Now all turn over your booklets to look at the back page. On this page you can see some questions which give you practice in how to enter your answers to the questions in the test. The first question is P1 and it has a passage about otter cubs. You have to read this passage, then decide how the sentence which follows should be completed to reproduce the sense of the passage. I will give you a minute to read the passage.

When the pupils have read the passage, say:

The question is about otter cubs when they are eight weeks old. Does the passage say that they learn to fish, that they are taught to hunt, that they swim for the first time, or that they leave their mother?

When the correct answer is called out, say:

That's right, the correct answer is that they swim for the first time, which is answer C, so we circle the letter C opposite P1.

This can be shown on the board if the practice section has been written-up in advance. You should demonstrate not only how to answer correctly, but also how to correct a wrong answer by rubbing it out and inserting the correct response. Tell the pupils that when inserting their answers they should make pencil marks which are heavy enough to be read easily, but not so heavy that they cannot be rubbed out if necessary. The marks

should therefore be clear but not heavily impressed.

Then say:

Now let's look at the next question, P2. This says 'One word in this sentence is in bold type. Choose the word which means most nearly the same. Circle A, B, C or D to show your answer.'

*P2 If you can be **obstinate**, so can I.*

A arrogant   **B** clever
C inquisitive   **D** stubborn

What is the correct answer to this?

When the correct answer is called out, say:

That's right, the correct answer is 'stubborn', which is answer D, so we circle the letter D opposite P2.

Again, this can be demonstrated on the board if the practice section has been drawn in advance. Then say:

Now let's look at the third question, P3. This has a passage about a girl called Kate. You have to read this passage, then look at the statement which follows and decide whether the passage agrees with it, disagrees with it or doesn't say. I will give you a minute to read the passage.

When the pupils have read the passage, say:

The sentence says 'Kate went upstairs in a hurry'. Does the passage agree, disagree, or doesn't it say?

When the correct answer is called out, say;

That's right, the passage agrees with the sentence, which is answer A, so we circle the letter A opposite P3.

When you are satisfied that the pupils understand what is required, proceed to the test itself. Say:

When you start the test itself, answer the questions in the same way you did for the practice questions. There are five sections to this test. When you reach the end of a section or the end of a page, go straight on to the next without waiting to be told. If you find that you cannot do a question, do not worry about it or spend a lot of time trying to do it, simply leave it and go on to the next. **Try to answer as many questions as you can.** *You will have 45 minutes to do the test and I will tell you when there are 30 minutes left, when there are 15 minutes left and when there are 5 minutes left. Are there any questions before you start?*

Answer any queries which may arise and then say:

Open your booklets and begin now.

After 15 minutes say:

You have had 15 minutes and there are 30 minutes left.

After 30 minues say:

You have had 30 minutes and there are 15 minutes left.

After 40 minutes say:

You have had 40 minutes and there are 5 minutes left.

After 45 minutes say:

Stop now, please. I will collect the test booklets.

Marking ▷

1. In marking, use only the official answer key given in this manual.

2. To make the task of marking as quick and easy as possible, and to ensure maximum accuracy, deal with only one page at a time, and make a point of repeating mentally only the correct answers when comparing key and script.

3. The answers are spaced according to the questions in the test. Marking is made easier if the test booklet is folded back and placed in correct position alongside the answers in the key.

4. Follow the answer key without deviation, even if occasionally some other answer seems plausible. In that case, or where an answer is not clear, draw attention to the answer by a note on the front cover.

5. Award one mark for each correct answer; give no fractional marks.

6. If the method of answering differs from that asked for in the rubric, or shown in the key

(e.g. underlining an answer instead of circling), give credit if the content of the answer is correct. If a pupil has changed his answer, by alteration or by crossing out and writing the answer at the side, give credit if the final intention is clear, and the content of the answer is correct.

7. If more than one response is marked (except by way of alteration) where only one should be, give no credit.

8. The marks should be recorded on each page as it is marked, and totalled at the foot of the page. The page totals should then be totalled, for each subtest and for the test as a whole, and recorded in the boxes at the foot of the front cover.

9. The pupil's chronological age should also be written in the box marked CA; but before doing this, it is advisable to check that the date of birth has been given correctly. Note that ages should be in *years and completed months*: for example, a child born on 16 March 1989 and tested on 15 April 2002 is aged 13:0.

Note: A **Scorer/Profiler CD-ROM** is available to facilitate rapid, computerised conversion of pupils' subtest raw scores to quotients and reading ages, and to generate subtest profiles for each pupil as well as a range of class/group performance analyses: contact the publisher for details.

Answers

Section A

PAGE 3		
A1	**C**	£150
A2	**E**	01276 9294
A3	**B**	4 years
A4	**A**	2 years
A5	**C**	£400
A6	**A**	£70

PAGE 5		
A7	**D**	15
A8	**C**	saucepan
A9	**D**	40 minutes
A10	**E**	ham
A11	**B**	grated
A12	**B**	4 teaspoons
A13	**A**	coconut milk
A14	**B**	2
A15	**C**	saffron
A16	**E**	chapattis

Section B

PAGE 6

B1	E	raised
B2	A	contents
B3	C	evident
B4	D	precise
B5	B	benefit
B6	A	absurd
B7	E	questioned
B8	B	instant
B9	C	forecast
B10	D	privacy
B11	B	fate

PAGE 7

B12	C	unconcerned
B13	D	genuine
B14	A	combine
B15	C	consequences
B16	C	immersing
B17	D	suitable
B18	B	boring
B19	A	deceptive
B20	E	plotted
B21	D	lessen
B22	C	qualities
B23	C	prosper
B24	D	intricacy

Section C

C1	B	Disagrees
C2	B	Disagrees
C3	A	Agrees
C4	B	Disagrees
C5	A	Agrees
C6	C	Doesn't say

C7	C	Doesn't say
C8	A	Agrees
C9	A	Agrees
C10	B	Disagrees
C11	C	Doesn't say
C12	B	Disagrees
C13	C	Doesn't say
C14	B	Disagrees

Section C

C15	**C**	Doesn't say
C16	**A**	Agrees
C17	**B**	Disagrees
C18	**A**	Agrees
C19	**A**	Agrees
C20	**C**	Doesn't say

Section D

D1	**B**
D2	**A**
D3	**D**
D4	**A**
D5	**E**
D6	**C**
D7	**B**
D8	**D**

Section D cont.

D9   B

D10 D

D11 E

D12 F

D13 A

D14 E

D15 C

D16 B

D17 D

Section E

E1   **B**   a man's escape from attackers

E2   **D**   to hinder his pursuers

E3   **A**   he had not undone the catch

E4   **B**   make him forget his panic

E5   **D**   winter night

E6   **C**   stood and shook his fist

PAGE 14

E7	**D**	a Sunday
E8	**C**	east
E9	**D**	is probably house-bound
E10	**B**	the mobility she has lost
E11	**C**	told the wrong time
E12	**A**	the way people use their Sundays

PAGE 15

E13	**C**	how camels are adapted to their environment
E14	**D**	they swing their legs further than other animals
E15	**D**	they live in rougher country
E16	**B**	their toenails
E17	**C**	having toes flat on the ground

Total Scores: QUOTIENTS AND PERCENTILES

> The quotients, reading ages and subtest profiles described on the following pages can all be computer-generated using a *Scorer/Profiler CD-ROM*, available separately from the publishers. Teachers are nevertheless strongly advised to read these pages in order to understand fully what the different types of scores mean and how to interpret them.

CALCULATION AND INTERPRETATION

Total raw scores, obtained by adding together all the correct responses, are in some ways inadequate to provide clear information about the pupil's performance. Firstly, they do not relate the performance to any well-defined standard and, secondly, they do not make any allowance for age. For these reasons, it is desirable to convert the 'raw' obtained scores to **quotients**: socres which *do* indicate how well a pupil has performed relative to a given population and, in particular, to others of the same age.

Tables 1, 2 and 3 give quotients on the basis of data obtained from schools in England and Scotland (for details of the standardisation samples, see page 30). In these tables, raw scores are set against age in years and completed months. A pupil's quotient is the number at the intersection of the row for his total raw score with the column for his age. For example, an English pupil with a total score of 59 and an age of 13:0 has a quotient of 107.

Taking each pupil's total raw score and age, from the front cover of the test booklet, follow the procedure described above and record the quotient in the box provided on the test booklet.

These quotients indicate how well a pupil has done by relating his performance to that of other pupils of the same age. Technically, quotients are normally distributed with a mean of 100 and a standard deviation of 15; but it is best to interpret them as showing what percentage of pupils from the standardisation sample obtained a score no higher than that of the pupil in question.

Table 4 gives these percentages, known as **age-adjusted percentiles**, for each quotient value. Thus an English pupil with a total score of 59, an age of 13:0 and a quotient of 107 has an age-adjusted percentile of 68 – which indicates that 68% of pupils of the same age did no better than him. Similarly, an English pupil with a total score of 36 and an age of 12:0 has a quotient of 92 and hence an age-adjusted percentile of 30, indicating that 30% of pupils of the same age did no better than him.

Table 1   Quotients (England) for ages 11:7 to 14:6

AWARD 130+ FOR ALL SCORES IN THIS AREA

AGE IN YEARS AND COMPLETED MONTHS AT DATE OF TEST

Test score	11:7	11:8	11:9	11:10	11:11	12:0	12:1	12:2	12:3	12:4	12:5	12:6	12:7	12:8	12:9	12:10	12:11	13:0	13:1	13:2	13:3	13:4	13:5	13:6	13:7	13:8	13:9	13:10	13:11	14:0	14:1	14:2	14:3	14:4	14:5	14:6	Test score
90																																					90
89																																				130	89
88																																		130	130	129	88
87																																130	130	129	129	126	87
86																														130	130	129	129	126	126	124	86
85																											130	130	129	129	126	126	124	124	122	85
84																									130	130	129	129	126	126	124	124	122	122	120	84
83																							130	130	129	129	126	126	124	124	122	122	120	120	119	83
82																					130	130	129	129	126	126	124	124	122	122	120	120	119	119	118	82
81																			130	130	129	129	126	126	124	124	122	122	120	120	119	119	118	118	117	81
80																	130	130	129	129	126	126	124	124	122	122	120	120	119	119	118	118	117	117	116	80
79															130	130	129	129	126	126	124	124	122	122	120	120	119	119	118	118	117	117	116	116	115	79
78													130	130	129	129	126	126	124	124	122	122	120	120	119	119	118	118	117	117	116	116	115	115	114	78
77											130	130	129	129	126	126	124	124	122	122	120	120	119	119	118	118	117	117	116	116	115	115	114	114	113	77
76									130	130	129	129	126	126	124	124	122	122	120	120	119	119	118	118	117	117	116	116	115	115	114	114	113	113	112	76
75							130	130	129	129	126	126	124	124	122	122	120	120	119	119	118	118	117	117	116	116	115	115	114	114	113	113	112	112	112	75
74					130	130	129	129	126	126	124	124	122	122	120	120	119	119	118	118	117	117	116	116	115	115	114	114	113	113	112	112	112	112	111	74
73				130	130	129	129	126	126	124	124	122	122	120	120	119	119	118	118	117	117	116	116	115	115	114	114	113	113	112	112	112	111	111	111	73
72		130	130	129	129	126	126	124	124	122	122	120	120	119	119	118	118	117	117	116	116	115	115	114	114	113	113	112	112	112	112	111	111	111	110	72
71	130	129	129	126	126	124	124	122	122	120	120	119	119	118	118	117	117	116	116	115	115	114	114	113	113	112	112	112	112	111	111	111	110	110	109	71
70	129	126	126	124	124	122	122	120	120	119	119	118	118	117	117	116	116	115	115	114	114	113	113	112	112	112	112	111	111	111	110	110	109	109	108	70
69	126	124	124	122	122	120	120	119	119	118	118	117	117	116	116	115	115	114	114	113	113	112	112	112	112	111	111	111	111	110	110	109	109	108	108	107	69
68	124	122	122	120	120	119	119	118	118	117	117	116	116	115	115	114	114	113	113	112	112	112	112	111	111	111	111	110	110	109	109	108	108	107	107	106	68
67	122	120	120	119	119	118	118	117	117	116	116	115	115	114	114	113	113	112	112	112	112	111	111	111	111	110	110	109	109	108	108	107	107	106	106	105	67
66	120	119	119	118	118	117	117	116	116	115	115	114	114	113	113	112	112	112	112	111	111	111	111	110	110	109	109	108	108	107	107	106	106	105	105	105	66
65	119	118	118	117	117	116	116	115	115	114	114	113	113	112	112	112	112	111	111	111	111	110	110	109	109	108	108	107	107	106	106	105	105	105	105	104	65
64	118	117	117	116	116	115	115	114	114	113	113	112	112	112	112	111	111	111	111	110	110	109	109	108	108	107	107	106	106	105	105	105	105	104	104	103	64
63	117	116	116	115	115	114	114	113	113	112	112	112	112	111	111	111	111	110	110	109	109	108	108	107	107	106	106	105	105	105	105	104	104	103	103	102	63
62	116	115	115	114	114	113	113	112	112	112	112	111	111	111	111	110	110	109	109	108	108	107	107	106	106	105	105	105	105	104	104	103	103	102	102	101	62
61	115	114	114	113	113	112	112	112	112	111	111	111	111	110	110	109	109	108	108	107	107	106	106	105	105	105	105	104	104	103	103	102	102	101	101	101	61
60	114	113	113	112	112	112	112	111	111	111	111	110	110	109	109	108	108	107	107	106	106	105	105	105	105	104	104	103	103	102	102	101	101	101	101	100	60
59	113	112	112	112	112	111	111	111	111	110	110	109	109	108	108	107	107	106	106	105	105	105	105	104	104	103	103	102	102	101	101	101	101	100	100	99	59
58	112	112	112	111	111	111	111	110	110	109	109	108	108	107	107	106	106	105	105	105	105	104	104	103	103	102	102	101	101	101	101	100	100	99	99	98	58
57	112	111	111	111	111	110	110	109	109	108	108	107	107	106	106	105	105	105	105	104	104	103	103	102	102	101	101	101	101	100	100	99	99	98	98	97	57
56	111	111	111	110	110	109	109	108	108	107	107	106	106	105	105	105	105	104	104	103	103	102	102	101	101	101	101	100	100	99	99	98	98	97	97	97	56
55	111	110	110	109	109	108	108	107	107	106	106	105	105	105	105	104	104	103	103	102	102	101	101	101	101	100	100	99	99	98	98	97	97	97	97	96	55
54	110	109	109	108	108	107	107	106	106	105	105	105	105	104	104	103	103	102	102	101	101	101	101	100	100	99	99	98	98	97	97	97	97	96	96	95	54
53	109	108	108	107	107	106	106	105	105	105	105	104	104	103	103	102	102	101	101	101	101	100	100	99	99	98	98	97	97	97	97	96	96	95	95	94	53
52	108	107	107	106	106	105	105	105	105	104	104	103	103	102	102	101	101	101	101	100	100	99	99	98	98	97	97	97	97	96	96	95	95	94	94	94	52
51	107	106	106	105	105	105	105	104	104	103	103	102	102	101	101	101	101	100	100	99	99	98	98	97	97	97	97	96	96	95	95	94	94	94	94	93	51
50	106	105	105	105	105	104	104	103	103	102	102	101	101	101	101	100	100	99	99	98	98	97	97	97	97	96	96	95	95	94	94	94	94	93	93	92	50

16

AGE IN YEARS AND COMPLETED MONTHS AT DATE OF TEST

Test score	11:7	11:8	11:9	11:10 11:11	12:0	12:1	12:2	12:3	12:4	12:5	12:6	12:7	12:8	12:9	12:10	12:11	13:0	13:1	13:2	13:3	13:4	13:5	13:6	13:7	13:8	13:9	13:10 13:11	14:0	14:1	14:2	14:3	14:4	14:5	14:6	Test score
49	106	106	105	105	104	103	103	102	102	101	101	100	100	100	99	99	98	98	98	97	97	96	96	96	95	95	94	94	93	93	92	92	92	91	49
48	105	105	104	104	103	102	102	101	101	100	100	100	99	99	98	98	98	97	97	96	96	96	95	95	94	94	93	93	92	92	92	91	91	91	48
47	104	104	103	103	102	101	101	100	100	99	99	98	98	98	98	97	97	96	96	96	95	95	94	94	93	93	93	92	92	91	91	91	90	90	47
46	104	103	103	102	101	101	100	99	99	98	98	98	97	97	97	96	96	95	95	95	94	93	93	92	92	92	91	90	91	90	90	90	89	89	46
45	103	102	102	101	100	100	99	98	98	97	97	97	96	96	96	95	95	94	94	94	93	93	93	92	92	91	90	90	89	90	90	89	89	88	45
44	102	101	101	100	99	99	98	97	97	96	96	95	95	95	95	94	94	93	93	93	92	92	91	91	91	90	89	89	88	89	88	88	88	88	44
43	101	100	100	99	98	98	97	96	96	95	95	95	94	94	94	93	93	92	92	92	92	91	90	90	90	89	88	88	88	88	87	87	87	87	43
42	100	100	99	98	98	97	96	95	95	95	94	94	93	93	93	92	92	91	91	91	91	90	89	89	89	88	88	87	87	86	87	86	86	85	42
41	99	99	98	97	97	96	95	95	95	94	93	93	93	93	92	91	91	90	90	90	90	90	89	88	88	88	87	87	86	86	86	85	86	85	41
40	98	98	97	96	96	95	95	94	94	93	93	93	92	92	91	90	90	90	90	89	89	88	88	88	87	87	86	86	86	86	85	85	85	84	40
39	97	97	96	96	95	94	94	93	93	92	92	91	91	91	90	90	89	89	89	88	88	88	87	87	87	86	86	85	85	85	84	84	84	83	39
38	96	96	95	95	94	93	93	92	92	91	91	90	90	90	89	89	88	88	88	87	87	87	86	86	86	85	85	84	84	84	83	83	83	82	38
37	95	95	94	93	93	92	92	91	91	90	90	89	89	89	88	87	87	87	87	86	86	85	85	85	84	84	84	83	83	83	82	82	82	81	37
36	94	94	93	92	92	91	91	90	90	89	89	88	88	88	87	86	86	86	86	85	85	85	84	84	84	83	83	82	82	82	81	81	81	80	36
35	93	93	92	91	91	90	90	89	89	88	88	87	87	87	86	85	85	85	85	84	84	84	83	83	83	82	82	81	81	81	80	80	80	79	35
34	92	92	91	90	90	89	88	88	88	87	87	86	86	86	85	84	84	84	84	83	83	83	82	82	82	81	81	80	80	80	79	79	79	78	34
33	91	91	90	89	89	88	87	86	87	86	86	85	85	85	84	83	83	83	83	82	82	82	81	81	81	80	80	79	79	79	78	78	78	78	33
32	89	89	88	88	88	87	86	85	86	85	85	84	84	84	83	82	82	82	82	81	81	81	80	80	80	79	79	78	78	78	77	77	77	78	32
31	88	88	87	86	86	85	85	84	85	84	84	83	83	83	82	81	81	81	81	80	80	80	79	79	80	78	78	77	77	77	77	76	76	77	31
30	87	87	86	85	85	84	84	83	83	83	83	82	82	82	81	80	80	80	80	79	79	79	78	78	78	77	77	76	76	76	76	75	75	75	30
29	86	85	85	84	84	83	83	82	82	82	82	81	81	81	80	80	79	79	79	78	78	78	77	77	77	76	76	75	75	75	75	74	74	74	29
28	85	84	84	83	83	82	82	81	81	81	80	80	80	79	79	79	78	78	78	77	77	77	76	76	76	75	75	74	74	74	74	73	73	73	28
27	84	83	83	82	82	81	81	80	80	80	79	79	79	78	78	77	77	77	76	76	76	75	75	75	75	74	74	73	73	73	73	72	72	72	27
26	82	82	82	81	80	80	80	79	79	78	78	78	77	77	76	76	76	76	75	75	75	74	74	74	74	73	73	72	72	72	72	71	71	71	26
25	81	81	81	80	79	79	78	78	78	77	77	77	76	76	75	75	75	75	74	74	74	73	73	73	73	72	72	71	71	71	71	70	70	70	25
24	80	80	79	79	78	78	77	77	76	76	76	75	75	74	74	74	74	73	73	73	72	72	72	72	71	71	71	70	70	70	70	70	70		24
23	79	78	78	77	77	76	76	75	75	75	74	74	74	73	73	73	72	72	72	72	71	71	71	71	70	70	70	70	70						23
22	77	77	77	76	75	75	75	74	74	73	73	73	73	72	72	71	71	71	71	70	70	70	70	70				70	70						22
21	76	76	75	75	74	74	73	73	73	72	72	72	71	71	71	70	70	70	70	70	70	70					70	70	70						21
20	75	74	74	73	73	72	72	72	71	71	71	70	70	70		70	70	70	70	70	70	70													20
19	73	73	72	72	71	71	71	71	70	70	70																								19
18	72	71	71	70	70	70	70	70	70																										18
17	70	70	70	70	70			70																											17
16	70																																		16
15	70																																		15
14																																			14
13																																			13
12																																			12
11																																			11
10																																			10

AWARD 70— FOR ALL SCORES IN THIS AREA

Table 2 Quotients (England) for ages 14:6 to 16:6

AGE IN YEARS AND COMPLETED MONTHS AT DATE OF TEST

Test score	16:6	16:5	16:4	16:3	16:2	16:1	16:0	15:11	15:10	15:9	15:8	15:7	15:6	15:5	15:4	15:3	15:2	15:1	15:0	14:11	14:10	14:9	14:8	14:7	14:6	Test score
90	130	130	130	130	130	130	130	130																		90
89	128	128	128	128	129	129	129	129	130	130	130	130	130	130	130	130	130	130	130	130	130				130	89
88	125	125	126	126	126	126	127	127	127	127	128	128	128	128	129	129	129	129	129	130	130	130	130	130	129	88
87	122	122	123	123	123	124	124	124	125	125	125	125	126	126	126	126	126	127	127	127	127	128	128	128	126	87
86	118	119	119	120	121	121	122	122	122	123	123	123	123	124	124	124	124	124	125	125	125	125	124	126	126	86
85	116	116	117	118	118	119	119	120	120	120	121	121	121	122	122	122	123	123	123	123	123	124	124	124	124	85
84	114	114	115	115	116	116	117	118	118	118	119	119	120	120	120	121	121	121	121	122	122	122	122	123	122	84
83	112	113	113	114	114	114	115	115	116	117	117	117	118	118	119	119	119	120	120	120	120	120	120	120	120	83
82	111	111	112	112	113	114	113	114	114	115	115	116	116	117	117	117	118	118	118	119	119	119	119	119	119	82
81	109	109	110	110	111	111	112	112	113	113	114	114	115	115	115	116	116	117	117	118	118	118	118	118	118	81
80	108	108	109	109	110	110	111	111	112	112	113	113	114	114	114	115	115	116	116	116	117	117	117	117	117	80
79	107	107	108	108	109	110	110	110	111	111	112	112	113	113	114	114	114	115	115	115	116	116	116	116	116	79
78	106	106	107	107	108	109	109	109	110	110	111	111	112	112	113	113	113	114	114	115	115	115	115	115	115	78
77	105	105	105	106	107	107	108	108	109	109	110	110	110	111	111	112	112	113	113	113	114	114	114	114	114	77
76	104	104	104	105	105	106	106	107	107	108	108	109	109	110	110	110	111	111	112	112	112	113	113	113	113	76
75	103	103	103	104	104	104	105	105	106	106	107	107	108	108	109	109	110	110	110	111	111	112	112	112	112	75
74	102	102	102	103	103	103	104	104	105	105	105	106	106	107	107	108	108	109	109	110	110	110	111	111	112	74
73	101	101	101	102	102	103	103	103	104	104	104	105	105	106	106	107	107	107	108	108	109	109	110	110	111	73
72	100	100	100	101	101	102	102	102	103	103	103	104	104	105	105	105	106	106	106	107	108	108	108	109	110	72
71	98	99	99	100	100	101	101	101	102	102	102	103	103	104	104	104	105	105	105	106	106	107	107	108	109	71
70	97	98	98	99	99	100	100	100	101	101	102	102	102	103	103	103	104	104	104	105	105	106	106	107	108	70
69	96	97	97	98	98	99	99	99	100	100	101	101	101	102	102	102	103	103	103	104	104	105	105	106	107	69
68	95	96	96	97	97	98	98	98	99	99	100	100	100	101	101	102	102	102	103	103	103	104	104	105	106	68
67	94	95	95	96	96	97	97	97	98	98	99	99	100	100	100	101	101	101	102	102	102	103	103	104	105	67
66	94	94	94	95	95	96	96	96	97	97	98	98	99	99	99	100	100	100	101	101	102	102	102	104	105	66
65	93	94	94	94	95	95	95	96	96	96	97	97	98	98	99	99	100	100	100	100	101	102	102	103	104	65
64	93	93	94	94	94	95	95	95	96	96	97	97	98	98	98	99	99	99	100	100	101	101	101	102	103	64
63	92	92	93	93	93	94	94	94	95	95	96	96	97	97	98	98	98	99	99	99	100	100	101	101	102	63
62	91	92	92	93	93	93	94	94	94	95	95	95	96	96	97	97	97	98	98	99	99	99	100	100	101	62
61	91	91	91	92	92	92	93	93	94	94	94	95	95	95	96	96	97	97	97	98	99	98	99	100	101	61
60	90	90	91	91	91	92	92	92	93	93	93	94	94	94	95	95	96	96	96	97	97	98	98	99	100	60
59	90	90	90	91	91	91	92	92	92	93	93	93	94	94	95	95	95	96	96	96	97	97	97	98	99	59
58	89	89	90	90	91	91	91	92	92	92	93	93	93	94	94	94	95	95	96	96	96	97	97	98	98	58
57	88	88	89	89	90	90	91	91	91	92	92	92	93	93	93	94	94	94	95	95	96	96	96	97	97	57
56	87	87	88	88	89	89	90	90	91	91	91	92	92	92	93	93	93	94	94	94	95	95	95	96	97	56
55	86	86	87	87	88	88	89	89	90	90	91	91	91	92	92	92	93	93	93	94	94	94	95	95	96	55
54	85	85	86	86	87	87	88	88	89	89	90	90	91	91	92	92	92	92	93	93	93	94	94	94	95	54
53	84	84	85	85	86	86	87	88	88	89	89	89	90	90	91	91	91	92	92	92	93	93	93	94	94	53
52	83	83	84	84	85	85	86	87	87	88	88	89	89	89	90	90	90	91	91	92	92	92	93	93	94	52
51	82	83	83	84	84	85	85	86	86	87	87	88	88	89	89	89	90	90	90	91	91	91	92	92	93	51
50	81	82	82	83	83	84	84	85	85	86	86	87	87	88	88	89	89	89	90	90	90	91	91	91	92	50

AGE IN YEARS AND COMPLETED MONTHS AT DATE OF TEST

Test score	16:6	16:5	16:4	16:3	16:2	16:1	16:0	15:11	15:10	15:9	15:8	15:7	15:6	15:5	15:4	15:3	15:2	15:1	15:0	14:11	14:10	14:9	14:8	14:7	14:6	Test score
49	81	81	81	82	82	83	83	84	84	85	85	86	86	87	87	88	88	89	89	89	90	90	90	91	91	49
48	80	80	81	81	82	82	83	83	84	84	85	85	86	86	87	87	87	88	88	89	89	89	90	90	91	48
47	79	80	80	80	81	81	82	82	83	83	84	84	85	85	86	86	87	87	88	88	88	89	89	89	90	47
46	79	79	79	80	80	80	81	81	82	82	83	83	84	84	85	85	86	86	87	87	88	88	88	89	89	46
45	78	78	79	79	79	80	80	80	81	81	82	82	83	83	84	85	85	86	86	86	87	87	88	88	88	45
44	77	78	78	78	79	79	79	80	80	81	81	82	82	83	83	84	84	85	85	86	86	87	87	87	88	44
43	77	77	77	78	78	78	79	79	79	80	80	81	81	82	82	83	83	84	84	85	85	86	86	87	87	43
42	76	77	77	77	77	78	78	78	79	79	79	80	80	81	81	82	82	83	83	84	85	85	85	86	86	42
41	76	76	76	77	77	77	77	78	78	78	79	79	79	80	80	81	81	82	82	83	84	84	85	85	85	41
40	75	75	76	76	76	76	77	77	77	78	78	78	79	79	80	80	80	81	82	82	83	83	84	84	84	40
39	75	75	75	75	76	76	76	76	77	77	77	78	78	78	79	79	80	80	81	81	82	82	83	83	83	39
38	74	74	75	75	75	75	75	76	76	76	77	77	77	78	78	78	79	79	80	80	81	81	82	82	82	38
37	74	74	74	74	74	75	75	75	75	76	76	76	77	77	77	78	78	78	79	79	80	80	81	81	81	37
36	73	73	73	74	74	74	74	74	75	75	75	76	76	76	77	77	77	78	78	78	79	79	80	80	80	36
35	72	73	73	73	73	73	74	74	74	74	75	75	75	76	76	76	77	77	77	78	78	78	79	79	79	35
34	72	72	72	72	73	73	73	73	73	74	74	74	74	74	75	75	76	76	76	77	77	78	78	78	78	34
33	71	72	72	72	72	72	72	73	73	73	73	73	74	74	74	75	75	75	76	76	76	77	77	78	78	33
32	71	71	71	71	72	72	72	72	72	72	73	73	73	73	74	74	74	74	75	75	75	76	76	77	77	32
31	70	71	71	71	71	71	71	71	72	72	72	72	72	73	73	73	73	74	74	74	75	75	75	76	76	31
30	70	70	70	70	70	70	70	71	71	71	71	71	72	72	72	72	73	73	73	73	74	74	74	75	75	30
29					70	70	70	70	70	70	71	71	71	71	71	72	72	72	72	73	73	73	73	74	74	29
28								70	70	70	70	70	70	70	71	71	71	71	72	72	72	72	73	73	73	28
27												70	70	70	70	70	70	71	71	71	71	72	72	72	72	27
26																	70	70	70	70	70	71	71	71	71	26
25																			70	70	70	70	70	70	70	25
24																										24
23																										23
22																										22
21																										21
20																										20
19																										19
18																										18
17																										17
16																										16
15																										15
14																										14
13																										13
12																										12
11																										11
10																										10
	16:6	16:5	16:4	16:3	16:2	16:1	16:0	15:11	15:10	15:9	15:8	15:7	15:6	15:5	15:4	15:3	15:2	15:1	15:0	14:11	14:10	14:9	14:8	14:7	14:6	

AWARD 70– FOR ALL SCORES IN THIS AREA

19

Table 3   Quotients (Scotland) for ages 13:2 to 14:1

Test score	13:2	13:3	13:4	13:5	13:6	13:7	13:8	13:9	13:10	13:11	14:0	14:1	Test score
90													90
89													89
88													88
87													87
86				AWARD 120+ FOR ALL SCORES IN THIS AREA									86
85													85
84													84
83										120	120	120	83
82								120	120	119	119	119	82
81					120	120	120	119	119	118	118	117	81
80			120	120	119	119	118	118	117	117	117	116	80
79	120	120	119	119	118	118	117	117	116	116	115	115	79
78	119	118	118	117	117	116	116	115	115	114	114	113	78
77	117	117	116	116	115	115	115	114	114	113	112	112	77
76	116	115	115	115	114	114	113	113	112	112	111	110	76
75	115	114	114	114	113	113	112	112	111	110	110	109	75
74	114	113	113	113	112	112	111	110	110	109	109	108	74
73	113	113	112	112	111	111	110	109	109	108	108	108	73
72	112	112	111	111	110	110	109	108	108	108	107	107	72
71	111	111	110	110	109	109	108	108	107	107	106	106	71
70	110	110	109	109	108	108	107	107	106	106	105	105	70
69	109	109	108	108	107	107	106	106	105	105	105	104	69
68	108	108	107	106	106	106	105	105	104	104	104	103	68
67	107	106	106	105	105	105	104	104	104	103	103	103	67
66	106	105	105	105	104	104	104	103	103	103	102	102	66
65	105	104	104	104	104	103	103	103	102	102	101	101	65
64	104	104	103	103	103	103	102	102	101	101	101	100	64
63	103	103	103	102	102	102	101	101	101	100	100	100	63
62	103	102	102	102	101	101	101	100	100	100	99	99	62
61	102	102	101	101	101	100	100	100	99	99	98	98	61
60	101	101	101	100	100	100	99	99	98	98	98	97	60
59	101	100	100	100	99	99	99	98	98	97	97	97	59
58	100	100	99	99	99	98	98	97	97	97	96	96	58
57	99	99	99	98	98	98	97	97	96	96	95	95	57
56	99	98	98	98	97	97	96	96	96	95	95	94	56
55	98	98	97	97	96	96	96	95	95	94	94	94	55
54	97	97	97	96	96	95	95	95	94	94	93	93	54
53	97	96	96	95	95	95	94	94	93	93	93	92	53
52	96	96	95	95	94	94	94	93	93	92	92	91	52
51	95	95	94	94	94	93	93	92	92	92	91	91	51
50	95	94	94	93	93	93	92	92	91	91	90	90	50
49	94	93	93	93	92	92	91	91	91	90	90	89	49
48	93	93	92	92	92	91	91	90	90	89	89	88	48
47	92	92	92	91	91	90	90	89	89	88	88	87	47
46	92	91	91	90	90	89	89	88	88	87	87	87	46
45	91	91	90	90	89	88	88	87	87	87	86	86	45
44	90	90	89	89	88	87	87	86	86	86	85	85	44
43	89	89	88	87	87	86	86	85	85	85	85	84	43
42	88	87	87	86	86	85	85	85	84	84	84	84	42
41	87	86	86	85	85	84	84	84	84	83	83	83	41
40	85	85	84	84	84	83	83	83	83	83	83	82	40
39	84	84	83	83	83	83	82	82	82	82	82	82	39
38	83	82	82	82	82	82	82	81	81	81	81	81	38
37	81	81	81	81	81	81	81	81	81	81	81	81	37
36	80	80	80	80	80	80	80	80	80	80	80	80	36
35													35
34													34
33						AWARD 80− FOR ALL SCORES IN THIS AREA							33
32													32
31													31
30													30
	13:2	13:3	13:4	13:5	13:6	13:7	13:8	13:9	13:10	13:11	14:0	14:1	

AGE IN YEARS AND COMPLETED MONTHS AT DATE OF TEST

Quotient	70	71	72	73	74	75	76	77	78	79	80	81
Percentile	2	3	3	4	4	5	5	6	7	8	9	11
Quotient	82	83	84	85	86	87	88	89	90	91	92	93
Percentile	12	13	14	16	18	20	21	23	25	27	30	32
Quotient	94	95	96	97	98	99	100	101	102	103	104	105
Percentile	34	37	39	42	44	47	50	53	56	58	61	63
Quotient	106	107	108	109	110	111	112	113	114	115	116	117
Percentile	66	68	70	73	75	77	79	80	82	84	86	87
Quotient	118	119	120	121	122	123	124	125	126	127	128	129
Percentile	88	89	91	92	93	94	95	95	96	96	97	97

Table 4 Age-adjusted percentiles for each quotient score

Age-adjusted percentiles and quotients can be derived directly from each other and it may be wondered why both are given. The difference is that, while the quotients are not so immediately interpretable, they are distributed according to what is reasonably supposed to be the actual distribution of (presently realised) ability. Thus most pupils obtain quotients fairly close to the mean of 100 – 50% of them between 90 and 110 – while far fewer pupils obtain scores at either extreme. This corresponds to the common observation that more pupils are found at average levels of ability than are found at levels either far above or far below the average.

The use of quotients is intended to ensure that a difference of one point should roughly represent a constant difference in ability, at whatever level of score or ability it occurs. A change of one point in an age-adjusted percentile, in contrast, corresponds to a bigger change in reading ability at the extremes of attainment than it does in the middle.

CAUTIONS

The quotient a pupil receives measures his general reading performance at the time that the test is administered. It is based on his performance in the various tasks included in the test which sample different aspects of his present reading ability. The quotient does *not* indicate a child's *potential* capacity for reading, and it sets no limits to his possible improvement. A low quotient is a challenge to the teacher, a high quotient an encouragement; neither prophesies the future with certainty.

The scores from all tests are liable to error. Much the most reliable results from the present test are those for the whole test; but, even here, some allowance must be made. It is probable that a pupil's true quotient is slightly closer to 100 than is the one he actually obtains, so that a high

quotient is probably an over-estimate and a low quotient an under-estimate. But, on the average, it is reasonable to think of a pupil's 'true' quotient as probably lying within *plus or minus 4 points* of the quotient he actually obtains.

Interpreted in relation to the whole population, high and low quotients are likely to be exaggerated for a further reason. The test was standardised in mainstream classes in state secondary schools. But schools in the independent sector may well contain a higher proportion of very good readers, so a high quotient possibly *over*-estimates a pupil's performance in relation to the *total* school population, state and independent. On the other hand, the exclusion of special schools and remedial classes must lead to a low quotient *under*-estimating a pupil's general standing. The inability of the test to give accurate measurements above and below certain points is reflected in the curtailment of quotients above 130 and below 70 (120 and 80 in Table 3).

A group test is not suitable for determining a pupil's needs for special education. All pupils not qualifying for a quotient of 70 should therefore be recorded as having obtained 70−; but this should be taken as a recommendation for individual testing, by a special needs coordinator or an educational psychologist, and not as an ultimate judgement of the pupil's serious backwardness in reading.

Finally, it must be recognised that any table of quotients relates a pupil's performance to that of a particular sample of children. Care was taken in the selection of samples for this standardisation to get as fair as possible a representation of the English state school population in 1999. Clearly the results are likely to fit other populations less well, including the corresponding ones from England in later years. Thus changes in reading standards may gradually render the standardisation inaccurate.

Reading Ages

The quotients obtained from Tables 1, 2 and 3 relate a pupil's performance to that of others of the same age. Another way of placing a pupil's performance is to relate it to the age at which such a performance is typical. This is the method of **reading ages**. A pupil's reading age indicates that he is reading as well as the *average* pupil of that age.

Reading ages are calculated by finding, for each age group, the mid-score – i.e. that score which divides their results 50:50. Then any pupil, whatever his actual age, who obtains a certain mid-score is said to have a reading age equal to the chronological age of the group to which it belongs.

A limiting factor in providing reading ages is the need to test children outside the age-range for which the test is really intended: only then can they be calculated for the brighter older pupil or the less bright younger one. But in the present standardisations, all but a few of the pupils tested were within the age range 11:7 to 16:6 (England) and 13:2 to 14:1 (Scotland).

Well-founded reading ages can only be given, therefore, for these ranges – see Tables 5 and 6.

Raw Score	Reading Age	Raw Score	Reading Age
39	*11:00*	58	14:01
40	*11:02*	59	14:03
41	*11:04*	60	14:05
42	*11:06*	61	14:07
43	11:08	62	14:08
44	11:10	63	14:09
45	12:00	64	14:11
46	12:02	65	15:00
47	12:04	66	15:02
48	12:06	67	15:05
49	12:08	68	15:07
50	12:10	69	15:09
51	13:00	70	16:00
52	13:02	71	16:02
53	13:03	72	16:05
54	13:05	*73*	*16:07*
55	13:07	*74*	*16:10*
56	13:09	*75*	*17:00*
57	13:11		

Table 5   English reading ages

Raw Score	Reading Age
58	13:2
59	13:4
60	13:6
61	13:8
62	13:10
63	14:0
64	14:1

Table 6   Scottish reading ages

Using the Subtest Scores

Each of the five subtests is intended to measure a particular aspect of reading competence. Interpretation of the subtest scores requires considerable caution, however.

In this revision of **Edinburgh Reading Test 4**, the time allocated for the test as a whole is limited, but pupils do not have to move from one subtest to the next at set points. This greatly simplifies the administration of the test, but it does mean that pupils' scores on each subtest will depend not only on their attainment on the skills measured by that subtest, but also on how they have divided their time *between* the subtests. In particular, a very low score on subtests D or E may indicate not that the pupil is poor at Points of View or Comprehension, but that he spent most (or even all!) of the 45 minutes on the first three subtests. Similarly, a very high score on subtest A may mean not that the pupil is very good at Skimming, but that he spent enough time on subtest A to guarantee getting most items right, possibly at the cost of suppressed scores on later subtests.

It is therefore necessary to interpret all five subtest scores together, as the profile of scores contains information about how the pupil used the 45 minutes, as well as about his strengths and weaknesses in reading. In particular, if a pupil's score on subtest D or E is markedly lower than his scores on earlier subtests, it may be worth checking the pupil's actual responses to verify how many questions he attempted.

Only if there is evidence that the low score was indeed due to incorrect answers should it be interpreted as possible evidence of weakness in these skills.

Even if later items have not been attempted, however, the pupil's overall score on the test remains a valid measure of overall reading ability, since scoring well on the test requires a combination of speed as well as power, and this combination is accurately measured by the total number of items answered correctly in a set time.

Subtest scores should be used only to make comparisons between different aspects of an individual pupil's performance, and *not* to compare his performance with that of other pupils. For each pupil, the decision to be made is whether the pupil's score for each subtest is unusually high or low *with respect to that pupil's score on the test as a whole.* This can be determined by reference to Table 7.

First locate the appropriate row in the table by finding in the first column the pupil's total raw score on the whole test. The other entries in that row give the range of raw scores for each subtest which would be expected for a pupil with a whole test score in that range. A subtest score outside the range can be regarded as unusually high or low, and should be noted in the score panel on the front cover of the pupil's test booklet (tick *high* or *low*, as appropriate).

Score on whole test	Subtest A range	Subtest B range	Subtest C range	Subtest D range	Subtest E range
15–19	7–15	0–5	2–10	0–4	0–4
20–24	8–16	0–7	3–11	0–5	0–5
25–29	8–16	0–9	4–12	0–6	0–6
30–34	9–16	1–10	5–13	0–7	0–8
35–39	9–16	2–12	6–14	0–8	0–9
40–44	10–16	4–13	7–15	1–9	0–10
45–49	10–16	5–15	8–16	2–10	1–11
50–54	11–16	7–17	9–17	3–11	2–12
55–59	11–16	9–18	9–18	4–12	3–13
60–64	11–16	10–20	10–19	5–13	4–14
65–69	11–16	12–21	11–20	6–14	5–15
70–74	12–16	13–23	12–20	7–15	6–16
75–79	12–16	15–24	13–20	8–16	7–17
80–84	13–16	17–24	14–20	9–17	8–17
85–89	13–16	18–24	15–20	10–17	9–17
90–94	14–16	20–24	16–20	11–17	10–17

Table 7 Expected subtest scores for each whole test score

It will be noted that Table 7 does not cover total raw scores of less than 15. This is because *unusually* low subtest scores are not possible for pupils whose whole test scores are as low as this, since their expected subtest scores are too low. Conversely, unusually high scores are not possible since they have not gained enough marks overall to have exceptionally high scores for any subtest.

These subtest results are not so reliable as the result for the whole test, because they are based on a smaller number of items. Great caution must be taken in their interpretation, therefore.

Small differences between a pupil's scores on the different subtests may well arise by chance.

Significance should not, therefore, be attached to every discrepancy.

When a subtest result is singled out as unusually high or low, the test is suggesting that this aspect of the pupil's ability should be looked at; but, even here, the teacher should not automatically accept the diagnosis, but should confirm it through her own observations. Also, the fact that a particular subtest score is singled out in this way does *not* mean that the teacher should pay no attention to the other results. The pattern of results may well suggest a meaningful interpretation of the pupil's difficulties in reading; but the pattern must not force an interpretation – as explained above, it may have arisen by chance.

Design of the Subtests

The general principle on which each subtest is constructed is that of isolating as far as possible the aspect of reading competence which it is designed to test. Thus each subtest has been made as easy as it could be in all dimensions except the one with which it is concerned. It might be expected, therefore, that the subtests would give markedly different assessments of a pupil, crediting him with distinctly greater competence in some aspects of reading than in others. The truth, however, with these subtests as with all other reading tests, is that they agree closely with each other about almost every pupil – that is, the subtests are highly correlated.

This means that reading can be thought of as a unified ability – an accomplishment which children tend to be good or bad at as a whole. By the time pupils have had some experience of secondary school, however, we may think in terms of different reading tasks as being more important than the skills defined for earlier Stages of the **Edinburgh Reading Tests** series. With the exception of vocabulary, there is at present insufficient evidence to distinguish *types* of reading comprehension, except in terms of a range of tasks which are commonly found. In general, different types of reading task are not taught in school, either as 'reading' or as study skills. Part of the purpose of a test such as this is to set both teachers and pupils thinking about how they use reading, both in various school subjects and in everyday life. Literacy is cross-curricular, and is not confined to English classes.

The warning against placing weight on every discrepancy does not have educationally undesirable consequences. The subtests can, through their separation of tasks, pick out pupils who do need special help in particular areas; and the procedure is not likely to under-estimate the relatively small number of pupils needing special, as well as general, help with their reading.

*Note: In discussing the subtests, the emphasis has so far been placed on the diagnosis of relative strengths or weaknesses that stand out from a pupil's general level of performance. As stated above, however, most pupils perform at much the same level on all tasks. They include pupils who are weak in reading, whatever aspect is considered. **These pupils need overall help to the same degree as others need help on their one weakness**. The suggestions that follow for support work on the subtests should* *all be taken to apply to pupils who are backward on reading as a whole.*

LOW SCORES ON THE SUBTESTS

First see whether the pupil has misunderstood the structure of the items or the form of response required. Determine also (except in the case of subtest A) whether the low score is a result of the pupil's not having attempted many items. If his other scores are good, his slowness may be due to a specific reaction to the subtest items. If, however, his other scores are average, it is extremely probable that the pupil's slowness does indicate a weakness in the relevant skill. Indeed, it is possible that his more basic skills are not sufficiently developed for a meaningful assessment to be made of the ability that the subtest seeks to measure.

Each pupil found to have an unusually low score on any subtest should be seen individually by the teacher, who should discuss the subtest with him at a time when she is free to give the pupil her full attention. Quite as much individual attention should be devoted to each pupil who has done poorly on the whole test (that is, at the very least, any pupil with a quotient of 85 or less). Though the teacher may not have time to go through all the subtests with him, particularly if the class contains several such pupils, this would be the most desirable and advantageous course of action.

The explicit aim must be to 'find out what he found difficult', and there must be no hint of criticism. Otherwise a pupil may become defensive and valuable diagnostic information will be lost. Sit down with the pupil, giving him a blank copy of the test open at a subtest on which he did badly. If this subtest result was exceptional for him, tell him that he did very well on most parts of the test; if he has done poorly throughout the test, reassure him that you are pleased with the way that he tackled the test. Then say that you want to go over this part of the test with him.

Ask him first whether he found it difficult. If he says 'No', give him a minute or two to recall the section and then ask him to show you any parts he found difficult. Get him to read the instructions aloud. Note any errors, but do not clarify them for him at this stage. Get him to answer the subtest items, asking him to read them aloud and noting any errors in his reading. Notice if he is following the instructions correctly and, if not, explain them to him at this point. If he is very slow, try to find out what is puzzling him. If he gets an answer wrong, ask him why he thinks his answer is right. Look for failure not only in the sub-skill being tested, but also in word recognition and in keeping a grasp on the nature of the task. This will show whether the pupil is deficient in the sub-skill, or whether some other feature of this particular set of items caused him difficulty.

Rationale of the individual Subtests

SUBTEST A: SKIMMING

The objective here is to test the pupil's ability to select appropriate responses without the benefit of contextual clues in the passage. The 16 items in general are not intended to present any special difficulty, beyond the general location of a word or phrase in the text.

Unusually low scores

A discrepant score is much more likely to be singled out on this subtest than on any other. Less weight should be placed on such a score, however, because it may be that the pupils are unfamiliar with material of this type and did not grasp the object of the subtest. However, there is little scope for 'informed' guessing, and wrong answers are relatively rare.

If a pupil answers very few questions, then there is little doubt that he has not yet learned the skill of 'skimming'. This is an important skill, if a pupil has to read a great deal, or read it quickly, or, for instance, if one has to check quantities, or locate a particular small advertisement. It is not, however, a skill that can readily be taught – although awareness of the technique is helpful, and cloze procedure may be useful.

If, on the other hand, a pupil produces a number of wrong responses, this is an altogether different – and much rarer – problem. Clearly, such a pupil is a careless or inaccurate reader, and practice in the use of context is probably helpful. We all guess on the basis of more or less inadquate evidence, but the reader who does not know when the evidence is insufficient is probably having problems at a much lower level.

SUBTEST B: VOCABULARY

This subtest sets out to measure the essential skill by which our vocabulary is built up: the ability to select for a given context – from a number of alternatives, more or less plausible in context – the word that means most nearly the same as a 'problem' word. The 24 items are all of the same type, confronting pupils with nouns, verbs and adjectives of progressively increasing difficulty, for which they have to find synonyms. In doing items of this type, the pupil must select from amongst five alternatives –

each of which *could* fit the sentence both grammatically and semantically – the only one which will mean the same in context as the underlined word. The meaning of the latter must be firmly held in mind while each of the possibilities is tested against it.

Unusually low scores

In this subtest, as in each of the others, an unusually low score implies a contrast with the pupil's performance on the other subtests. We have here, then, a pupil who succeeds well enough in handling the structures of written language and in understanding connected writing, but who is comparatively deficient in the recognition or understanding of individual words. In general, such pupils will benefit from an enriched linguistic diet, and encouragement to explore the resources of the language in their own writing. They can be led, by discussion, to see how a single word can condense and summarise the meaning of an extended phrase, exploring use of shades of meaning (near-synonyms), to express oneself more precisely, and the use of categories, metaphors and similes. Useful teaching points might arise from discussion of what *makes* wrong choices wrong.

Unusually high scores

An unusually high score on this, as on the other subtests, is encouraging, suggesting that the pupil could well be brought up to the same standard in all aspects of reading ability. Here vocabulary is apparently available to underpin reading competence. Therefore, attention can be concentrated on any subtest scores which are unusually low, and material provided that involves more complex structures and a wide variety of reading tasks, and understanding of various kinds, while building on the strong basis of vocabulary.

SUBTEST C: READING FOR FACTS

This subtest calls for a rather more developed skill than does subtest A. It involves a task which is much closer to *understanding*: the ability to discuss what a passage says or does not say. This may seem dull, but a large part of the value of reading, after the momentary pleasure, lies in what can be retained. Moreover, where the reader does not take sufficient care, entirely the wrong impression can be carried away, simply because the reader expects a particular conclusion, or has his expectation reinforced by certain words being close to each other. Understanding what is read can, on occasion, be a question of sorting out fact from expectation.

Most of the 20 items in this section – for example C1, C3, C4, C7, C11, C13 and C20 – are quite explicit. That is, they either agree or disagree with the passages in the same form of words, or one very close; or the passage makes no mention whatever of the item. Some, however, of the 'doesn't say' category have 'red-herring' appearances of the key words of the item within the text – for example, C6. Similarly, some of the 'agrees' and 'disagrees' items require the pupils to deal with synonyms or, alternatively, with oblique allusions – such as C8, C9 (synonyms), C2, C5, C10, C12, C14, C16 and C17 (oblique references). These are of various types, and do not form a homogenous sub-group.

Unusually low scores

Consider first whether the pupil's low score may be attributed to anxiety. If this can be discounted, encourage the pupil actively to consider whether he is, in his reading, extracting as much relevant information as necessary: encourage him to consider what he has read more carefully, and ask himself questions about it, rather than simply assume that he has understood it properly. His performance may also be improved by exercises using cloze procedure.

Unusually high scores

An unusually high score on this subtest may be a very promising sign that the pupil is developing a 'critical faculty' – the ability to get at the writer's meaning, and not to be misled either by what the author tries to conceal or by misleading modes of expression, or random collections of ideas. He is therefore likely to be well fitted to develop other reading skills. This is especially true of a younger pupil, or one from a disadvantaged background.

SUBTEST D: POINTS OF VIEW

The 17 items in this subtest were designed to assess the pupil's ability to connect together, using both 'ideological' and 'personality' clues, groups of ideas which 'hang together'.
Page 11: Argument A is based on the separation

of labour and wealth, and possibly a little envy on the part of the speaker. If this is observed, the argument is immediately conspicuous; none of the others display this particular emotion.

Argument B is simple. It disregards politics, makes no mention of loyalty, morality or social justice, and enjoys the spectacular qualities of the Royal Family.

Arguments C, D and E all concentrate on different aspects of the Royal Family as a focal point: argument C on Royalty as an object of loyalty and communal feeling; argument D on the royal power over parliament – which is, in a sense, fallacious, of course – and argument E on the moral supremacy which the speaker believes them to possess. In order to deal with these arguments, the pupil must be able clearly to separate the moral from the political, and to make very precise categories, without necessarily taking into account the rightness of the opinion.

Page 12: Argument A is, in a sense, on its own. It has 'emotional' links with argument F, in that A is denouncing a road-builders' 'lobby', where F is the heavy road-user speaking; but A is the case against, whereas F is the case for. Similarly, C is the 'economic' case for better communication, and E represents the unreflecting private drivers. Therefore, the pupil has to distinguish between these arguments on the basis of the speaker's immediate interest: he must categorise the road-building, the lorry-driver, the car-driver, and the 'impartial' economist, and bear these distinctions in mind. It is also necessary to distinguish the conventional economic case for roads from the case against, which in this instance is based upon the ultimate exhaustion of scarce natural resources.

Thus, the pupil must distinguish not just the category into which the speaker falls, but also *where* in that category, and select the internally-consistent groups. Finally, he has to distinguish between argument D, which is based on the apparent impossibility of maintaining our present type of economic activity, and argument B, which is the 'environmentalist' case, that one has to consider the full cost of the road – to the surroundings and in 'the quality of life'. Thus, the distinctions are finer than those on page 11.

Unusually low scores
Low scores on this subtest may be due to the pupil having progressed through the test as a

whole relatively slowly and hence not having attempted some or all of the Points of View items. A pupil who has failed on many of these items, however, should be asked whether he can write down what each of the speakers is arguing. If he can do this successfully, ask him to compare other statements that might be uttered by the same speaker. Clearly, if the intention is to use the test again subsequently to test progress, this procedure could be described as 'teaching to the test'. The objective, however, is to make the pupil conscious of how an argument can be built up.

The topics used in this subtest are convenient starting-points, nothing more. If several pupils have unusually low scores, it is worth considering whether enough is being done to encourage dicussion and debate in class, and particularly to encourage those with unusually low scores on this subtest to take part.

Unusually high scores

If a pupil scores well on this subtest when, in general, his scores are low, it suggests a special interest in the kind of controversy upon which it is based, or in the personal values of debate. This is something which can be exploited to motivate the pupil's overall performance, and encourage him to read material about topics in which he is interested, and to put down on paper arguments on various ideas.

If the pupil scores exceptionally well on this section, when his performance is satisfactory on other sections, it suggests that he knows clearly what he is interested in. While this presents no problems, in general, it should be verified and borne in mind.

SUBTEST E: COMPREHENSION

This subtest comprises 17 items based on three prose passages – two fiction and one factual. Pages 13 and 14 are 'literary', consisting of passages of narrative, whereas page 15 is more factual and expository, covering the characteristics of camels and other animals.

Items E1, E7 and E13 call upon the pupil's ability to recognise what is the gist of a passage, and to summarise in one sentence the main theme or the most important part of the subject-matter, while the other items are more concerned with individual phrases.

Items E3, E5 and E8 require an element of inference from what is given in the passage. There is no direct reference to the items in the passage, but the correct answers can be accurately inferred from the text. Items E11, E14, E15, E16 and E17 require a paraphrase of what the passage says, and a large inferential element.

Unusually low scores

As for subtest D, low scores on this subtest may be due to the pupil not having attempted some or all of the Comprehension items. If this is not the reason, however, then where the low score is obtained by a pupil at the lower end of the age range, the teacher should take care that comprehension skills do develop, rather than think in terms of present remedy. For a younger pupil, the use of the test as teaching material is unlikely to be important, compared with an enrichment of the pupil's cognitive diet and encouragement to derive more from his reading. With an older pupil, however, the problem is more acute. It is necessary to confirm that his overall performance is unsatisfactory, before any action is contemplated. If his reading performance is unsatisfactory overall, then information must be gathered about the reasons for the pupil's unsatisfactory performance. Some information can be obtained by asking the pupil the reasons for choosing the responses that he did, and looking for the pattern in these responses.

Unusually high scores

Such a score is, of course, unusually encouraging, because the subtest is close to the central purpose of reading. Any subtest scores which are unusually low may be indications of those areas which are holding back the pupil's overall performance.

THE 2000 STANDARDISATION SAMPLES

Tables 1 and 3, for conversion of total raw scores to quotients, are based on the performance of two groups. One group consisted of 3181 pupils in seventeen state schools in England. The schools were located in Somerset, Yorkshire, Durham and Sussex. They were selected in such a way that, collectively, their profile of attainment in GCSE examinations closely matched the national profile for England as a whole. The elements of this profile, as published each year by the Department for Education and Skills, are (i) the proportion of fifteen-year-olds attaining five or more passes at A* to C; (ii) the proportion of fifteen-year-olds attaining five or more passes at A* to G; (iii) the proportion of fifteen-year-olds attaining one or more passes at A* to G, and (iv) the average points score. For more details of these profiles, see the Department for Education and Skills website: http://www.dfes.gov.uk/perform.htm.

The age distribution of these 3181 pupils, grouped into six-month bands, was as follows:

11:7–12:0	12:1–12:6	12:7–13:0	13:1–13:6	13:7–14:0	14:1–14:6
16.6%	15.9%	15.0%	15.2%	18.2%	19.0%

The other group consisted of 732 pupils from six schools in Stirling Council in Scotland. When compared on an age-for-age basis, the Scottish pupils scored on average about five marks higher than the English pupils. It is not possible to say whether this is because the Scottish schools were unrepresentative or because reading attainment is higher in Scottish schools, however, since data corresponding to the DfES tables do not exist in the same form in Scotland.

In any case, it was decided not to include the Scottish data in a single standardisation since they are not comparable and would distort the results. A separate table of norms (Table 3) was computed from the Scottish data, but it is limited (i) because the Scottish pupils covered a much smaller age range than the English pupils; (ii) because the smaller group size allowed the calculation of quotient scores only in the range 80–120 as opposed to 70–130; and (iii) because there is no evidence of the representativeness of the pupils in the group. Quotient scores derived from this table are probably acceptable as *Stirling* norms, since six out of seven secondary schools in Stirling Council took part, but they can only be regarded as *Scottish* norms in so far as Stirling is representative of Scotland. Of the 732 pupils, 48.5% were in the age range 13:2 to 13:7 and 51.5% in the age range 13:8 to 14:1.

It is hoped that, in due course, data from more Scottish schools will become available so that a standardisation table can be compiled which can be properly regarded as giving Scottish norms.

STANDARDISATION: TOTAL SCORES

The English standardisation of the whole test is based on the scores of all 3181 pupils in the sample between the ages 11:7 and 14:6. The Stirling standardisation is based on the scores of all 732 pupils between the ages 13:2 and 14:1. The conversion tables give deviation quotients (not mental-age type quotients) based on a normal distribution with a mean of 100 and a standard deviation of 15. The allowance for age is calculated on the basis of 13 linear regressions of score upon age at percentiles corresponding to quotients at 5-point intervals from 70 to 130 (9 linear regressions from 80 to 120 in Table 3). Intermediate quotients were obtained by linear interpolation.

READING AGES

Reading ages are based on the linear regression of score upon age at the 50th percentile. The data were of such a kind as to make extrapolation, to values outside the range of the standardisation group, inadvisable.

GENDER DIFFERENCES IN PERFORMANCE

Overall, as expected, in the standardisation sample girls performed slightly better than boys on this test. Figures based on the 3181 English pupils for the differences between sexes for each subtest and for the test as a whole are given in Table 8.

	Boys		Girls		All pupils	
	Mean	*Standard deviation*	*Mean*	*Standard deviation*	*Mean*	*Standard deviation*
Whole test	51.5	17.3	52.6	16.6	52.0	17.0
Subtest A	13.8	2.5	14.3	2.1	14.1	2.3
Subtest B	11.8	6.2	11.6	5.9	11.7	6.0
Subtest C	12.9	4.0	12.4	3.6	12.7	3.8
Subtest D	6.5	3.9	7.1	3.9	6.8	3.9
Subtest E	6.5	4.3	7.1	4.5	6.8	4.4

Table 8   Whole-test and subtest means and standard deviations, by gender

It was not considered appropriate at this age level to give separate norms for boys and girls. It was thought to be more desirable that pupils of either sex should be treated equally if their performance was equal, than that they should be treated equally according to their position within their own sex. A boy with a certain score should be regarded in the same light as a girl with that score, even though he has a higher standing among boys than she has among girls.

RELIABILITIES

Kuder-Richardson reliabilities (KR20) were calculated on the basis of the whole sample. The overall reliability of the test was 0.95. Separate reliabilities were also calculated for the five subtests. Their values, which are satisfactory, are:

Subtest	A	B	C	D	E
KR20 reliability	0.86	0.90	0.80	0.82	0.87

SUBTEST INTERCORRELATIONS

Product-moment correlations between the subtests were calculated on the basis of the raw scores from the whole sample. Their values are given in the table. The correlations are in general satisfactory, given the length and reliability of the subtests and distributions of their scores.

	A	B	C	D
B	0.46			
C	0.50	0.69		
D	0.40	0.72	0.63	
E	0.32	0.65	0.55	0.66

THE 2002 EXTENSION TO 16+

In this third edition of the manual, the tables for conversion of total raw scores to English quotients (standardised scores) and percentiles have been extended upwards to cover the ages from 14 years 7 months to 16 years 6 months, and reading ages to 17 years 0 months. Table 2 provides continuity from Table 1 across the full range of quotients.

This extension was based on the performance of 1442 children in the age range 14:7 to 16:6 tested in 2001. These children were drawn from eight secondary schools in England. These schools were mainly located in London and East Midlands. They were selected in such a way that, collectively, their profile of attainment in GCSE examinations closely matched the national profile for England as a whole (see page 30).

The ages of these children were distributed as shown below:

14:7–15:0	15:1–15:6	15:7–16:0	16:1–16:6
473	501	243	225